"As hard as it may be for their partisans to believe today, there was indeed a time when the Boston Red Sox did not exist. This flaw in the national culture was corrected in 1901."

—Donald Honig

101 Reasons
to Love the
Red Sox

David Green

Stewart, Tabori & Chang
New York

Introduction

I fell in love with baseball before I could read. Collecting baseball cards was my passion and I hoarded every penny and nickel I could scrounge until I reached the magic number of 10—enough to buy one pack of cards. I was in a euphoric state on days my mom took me to King's Drugs with 32 cents in my pocket, enough to purchase three packs of treasure, tax included. I hadn't yet started school so I had to get my older brother Ron to read the players' names to me and recite their teams and positions. I learned to know them by their faces and the team logos on their jerseys and caps.

Ron was already a die-hard Yankees fan at the age of eight. Of course Mickey Mantle, Ron's hero, was in his glory, and the Yankees were easy to like because they won on a regular basis. I, like most siblings, desperately wanted to emulate my older brother, but at the same time I was fiercely independent. I needed a team to call my own and, in 1967, I found it.

I was seven going on eight that summer. While the Twins, Tigers, White Sox and Red Sox waged an unforgettable battle for the pennant, I couldn't help but get caught up in the race, and my natural inclination to root for the underdog drew me to the Sox. I had the cards of all the stars—Yaz, Tony C, Jim Lonborg, Rico Petrocelli, and so on. The Sox won the pennant on the last day of the season, sweeping the Twins in a do-or-die two game series.

Next up was the mighty Cardinals in the World Series and a chance for the Sox to end nearly 50 years of frustration. But the Sox lost in seven games. I was crushed. I may have been a boy from North Carolina, but I had Red Sox blood.

In 1975, the Sox found themselves back in the World Series, this time facing the Cincinnati Reds. Carlton Fisk's heroic 12th-inning home run in Game 6 was followed by another crushing loss in Game 7. The attachment only deepened.

Then, Bucky "Bleepin" Dent in 1978. Game 6, 1986. And Aaron "Bleepin" Boone in 2003. How much could one team endure? Still, Red Sox Nation believed.

And, finally, in 2004, deliverance, bestowed by a team that never lost faith. First, the Sox dispatched the Yankees in historically glorious fashion — coming back to win four straight games after trailing in the ALCS three-games-to-none — thoroughly pounding them in Game 7. Then completely dominating the Cardinals in a World Series sweep.

This was a victory for so many. For Ted Williams, Bobby Doerr, and Johnny Pesky. For Carl Yastrzemski, Tony Conigliaro, and Jim Lonborg. For Carlton Fisk, Jim Rice, and Luis Tiant. For Bill Buckner, Bob Stanley, and Calvin Schiraldi. For Tom Yawkey, Dick O'Connell, and Harry Frazee. And for all the men who have worn the Red Sox uniform, and all the fans everywhere who have waited for so long, especially those whose days ended before this dream finally came true.

Red Sox Nation will never be the same. We now live in a wonderfully altered reality. The good guys have won, and we now have one more, HUGE, reason to love the Red Sox. The world is a better place.

See what happens when you believe.

1 Hope Springs Eternal

Every season fans across the country dream that this is their year—this will be the magical season when everything comes together and their team wins that elusive championship. Nowhere is this more true than in Boston, where Red Sox fans endured nearly 90 years of tragedy and frustration. To Red Sox fans, each and every new season begins full of hope and promise, and expectations of World Series glory—this is the year.

"The Red Sox are a religion. Every year we re-enact the agony and temptation in the Garden. Baseball's child's play? Well, up here in Boston, it's a passion play."

—George V. Higgins, *Time*

Player-manager Jimmy Collins preparing
to raise the 1903 championship flag

Ban Johnson

2 Red Sox Nation

With a fan base that reaches far beyond the confines of Fenway Park to include supporters throughout America, and all the world, this term is used to describe the fraternity of Red Sox faithful everywhere. Completely devoted despite 86 long years between titles, Red Sox Nation keeps the faith year after year.

3 Ban Johnson

Hired in 1894 as the president of the Western League, Johnson first rebuilt the midwestern minor league, then renamed it the American League and declared its "major league" status, positioning it in direct competition with the National League. On January 28, 1901, he announced the formation of the new American League franchise in Boston.

4 Huntington Avenue Grounds

Before they were known as the Red Sox, the Boston Americans, or Pilgrims as some referred to them, played in a ballpark known as the Huntington Avenue Grounds. The park officially opened on May 8, 1901, when Boston hosted the Philadelphia Athletics. The Beantown nine won 12–4, in a contest highlighted by an inside-the-park home run by Buck Freeman. The Grounds were built with several innovative features, including a covered lobby in which fans could wait out rain delays, showers for the players, and a locker room for the press. Boston won its first championship here and called the Huntington Avenue Grounds its home until Fenway Park opened in the spring of 1912.

Jimmy Collins

5 Five World Series Titles by 1918

The Red Sox won five world championships in their first 18 seasons, including four over a span of the years between 1912 and 1918.

6 Jimmy Collins

Despite being in the midst of a stellar career with the Boston Nationals when the American League was formed, Collins was the first player to sign a contract with the Boston Americans. He served as player-manager for the first six seasons, and recorded the team's first hit ever, a double, in the Red Sox' inaugural game versus Baltimore on April 26, 1901, later scoring the team's first run ever, on a hit by Buck Freeman. Under Collins, Boston recorded five straight winning seasons, two American League pennants, and its first world championship, in 1903.

"One man stood out above all others. No one would be more important to the success of the new team than the acknowledged star of the Bostons and the best player in the city, third baseman Jimmy Collins."

—Glenn Stout and Richard A. Johnson, *Red Sox Century*

7 The First Championship, 1903

The Red Sox won their first World Series in 1903, 5 games to 3 over a Pittsburgh team that featured Honus Wagner. Down 3 games to 1 and playing in Pittsburgh, the Red Sox took the next three games, then returned to Boston and won the clincher 3–0, behind Bill Dineen's second shutout and third victory of the series.

8 Bill Dineen

Though he didn't have a Hall of Fame career, in 1903 Dineen had as much to do with Boston's first world championship as anybody. He won 21 games during the regular season and followed that by going 3–1 in the World Series, pitching 35 innings with an ERA of 2.06. In the clinching victory, Dineen threw a shutout despite splitting open a finger on his pitching hand while fielding a ball in the third inning.

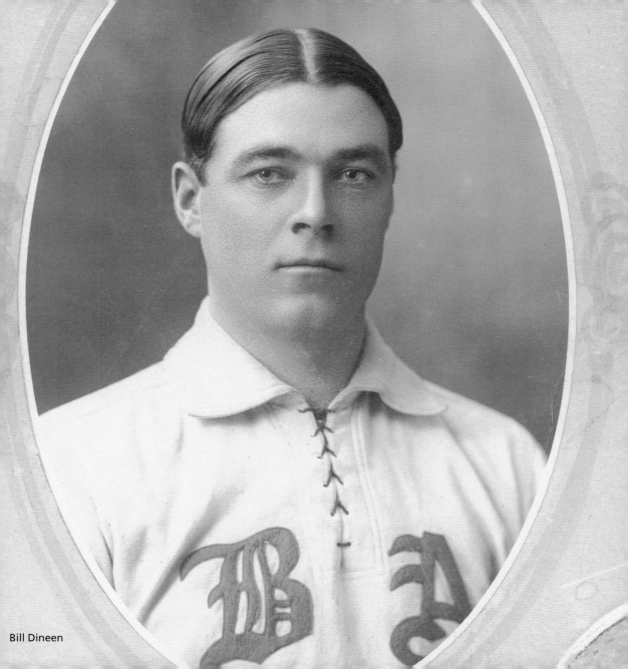

Bill Dineen

9 "Nuf Ced" McGreevey and the Royal Rooters

Michael T. "Nuf Ced" McGreevey was a local tavern owner and leader of the early Red Sox' most loyal and vocal band of supporters. Presiding over the baseball-obsessed denizens of his Roxbury tavern known as "3rd Base" because it was "the last stop before home," he declared an end to many a boisterous argument by slamming his fist onto the bar and announcing "nuf ced." His Royal Rooters followed the American League's Boston franchise with passion and devotion, often parading to the ballpark behind a band and singing vociferously during games.

10 Not This Time

On May 5, 1904, Cy Young pitched the first no-hitter and perfect game for the Boston Americans, beating the Philadelphia Athletics 3–0. Jesse Tannehill added a second "no-no" later that same year, and Boston pitchers have now tallied 16 in their 100-plus years, including two over the New York Yankees.

Boston clinched the American League pennant on the last day of the regular season, when they beat the New York Highlanders (Yankees) 3–2 in the first game of a doubleheader. No World Series was played that year, however. John T. Bush, owner of the National League champion New York Giants, refused to play a series versus Boston, denying them the opportunity to win a second straight world championship.

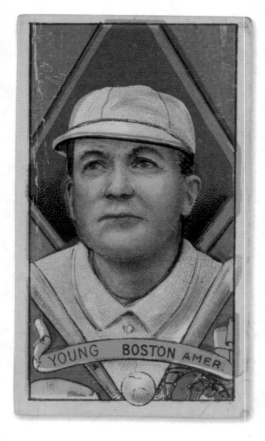

11 Cy Young

No other pitcher comes close to matching Denton True "Cy" Young's record of 511 wins, 749 complete games, and 7,356 innings pitched. Already well into his Hall of Fame career when he joined the Red Sox in 1901, Young had arguably his best season ever, posting a 33–10 record with an ERA of 1.62 and 158 strikeouts as the Sox finished second, four games behind the Chicago White Sox in their inaugural season. For eight years he anchored the Boston pitching staff, and led the team to its first world championship in 1903, winning two games in the World Series. On May 5, 1904, Young made history as he pitched the first perfect game ever recorded in the major leagues. Young won a total of 192 games for the Red Sox after joining them at the age of 34, all this while typically pitching on two days' rest.

"All us Youngs could throw. I used to kill squirrels with a stone when I was a kid, and my granddad once killed a turkey buzzard on the fly with a rock."

—Cy Young

Cy Young

12 The Red in Red Sox

A stunning crimson, it's the trademark color of the Sox. Beautifully rich, and alive, it appropriately represents both the deep, abiding love the fans have for their flawed team, and the legendary tragedies that have befallen the Sox throughout the team's history. Owner John I. Taylor chose the color in 1907 after the Boston Nationals cast aside their dark red stockings, deciding to wear blue instead, and the American League team from Boston became known as the Red Sox.

13 Shuttin' 'em Down

In 1906, Joe Harris pitched 24 innings in one game, including an American League record 20 consecutive scoreless innings, but lost 4–1 after giving up 3 runs in the top of the 24th.

14 Fenway Park

This is baseball heaven. No other ballpark has the feel and tradition of Fenway. Entering the grandstand, one is transported back through time as the spirits of all those who came before seem to still inhabit the cozy confines.

Built by Red Sox owner John I. Taylor, Fenway Park opened in the spring of 1912, just days after the *Titanic* sank. Though many changes have been made to Fenway Park over the years, the finely detailed brick facade that borders Yawkey Way dates to the first game played there.

15 Honey, Throw Me the Ball

The Red Sox won their first official game at Fenway 7–6, over the New York Highlanders (later known as the Yankees), on an RBI single by Tris Speaker. Boston mayor John "Honey Fitz" Fitzgerald threw out the first pitch. Five years later, Mayor Fitzgerald's grandson John F. Kennedy, the 35th president of the United States, was born.

"When they raze Fenway, it'll be like cutting down an old tree. Count the rings. There's one for each celebration and heartache suffered by Red Sox fans."

—Dan Shaughnessy

16 A Dream Season in 1912

From a 5–3 opening day victory in New York, and a 7–6
victory over the Highlanders in the first official game
played in Fenway Park, to a 3–2, 10th-inning victory over
the New York Giants in the final game of the World Series,
1912 was one of the greatest seasons ever in the Red Sox'
long and rich history. With a pitching staff anchored by
"Smoky" Joe Wood and a lineup that featured Tris Speaker,
Duffy Lewis, Harry Hooper, Larry Gardner, Heinie Wagner,
Steve Yerkes, Bill Carrigan, and Jake Stahl, the Red Sox ran
away with the pennant, finishing 105–47, then an American
League record, which included 14 straight victories over
the Highlanders.

The World Series once again went 8 games. Originally a
best-of-seven series, an eighth game was necessary when
Game 2 ended in a 6–6 tie, called because of darkness.
In the final game, the Red Sox bested New York 3–2 in
10 innings as Wood won his third game of the series, this
time in relief. In the fifth inning, Harry Hooper made a
miraculous over-the-shoulder bare-handed catch of a Larry
Doyle drive before tumbling over the right-field fence. Tris
Speaker drove in the tying run in the 10th after "Merkle's
Muff" and Larry Gardner followed a walk to Duffy Lewis
with a series-winning sacrifice fly.

"Smoky" Joe Wood, left, with Christy Mathewson

17 "Smoky" Joe Wood

Before joining the Red Sox in 1908, Wood first barnstormed with the Bloomer Girls, advertised as an all-female team that actually featured four male players. Though his first three seasons with Boston were unspectacular, "Smoky" Joe came into his own in 1911 when he won 23 games and pitched a no-hitter versus the St. Louis Browns. Wood's rise to greatness culminated in 1912 when he went a remarkable 34–5 with a 1.91 ERA and 258 strikeouts. On September 6 of that year, Wood brought his 13-game winning streak into a game versus the Washington Senators. Facing Walter Johnson, who had just had his record-setting 16-game winning streak snapped, Wood won the highly publicized battle 1–0, pitching a 6-hitter, and fashioned a 16-game winning streak of his own. He then won three games in the World Series including the clincher in a relief appearance as the Red Sox captured their second title.

18 "Merkle's Muff"

Trailing 2–1 with two on and one out in the bottom of the 10th in Game 8 of the 1912 World Series versus the Giants, Tris Speaker came to bat against the great Christy Mathewson. With the championship on the line, Speaker popped up in foul territory. Mathewson, first baseman Fred Merkle, and catcher Chief Meyers converged on the ball. Mathewson called for Meyers to make the play, even though Merkle had a better angle. Merkle pulled up short as Meyers unsuccessfully attempted to make the catch, and the ball fell between them. Given a second chance, Speaker then lined a hit into right field that scored Clyde Engle to tie the game, as Steve Yerkes advanced to third. After Duffy Lewis walked, Larry Gardner hit a long sacrifice fly, scoring Yerkes and giving the game and the series to Boston.

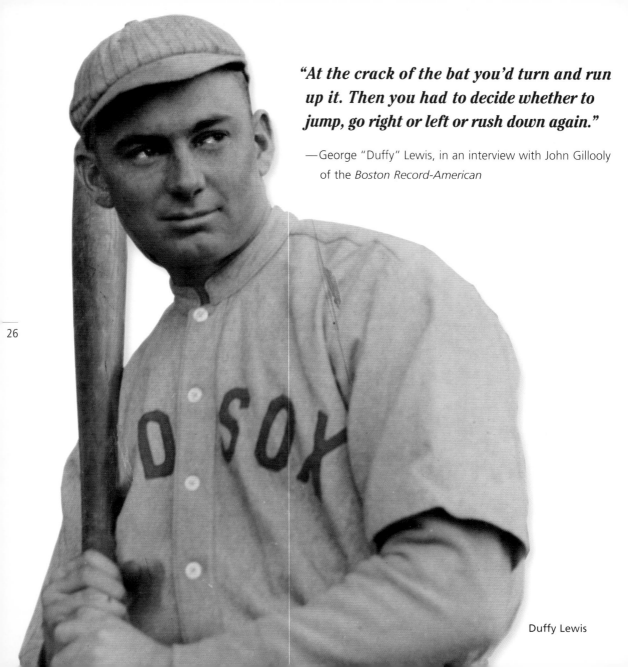

"At the crack of the bat you'd turn and run up it. Then you had to decide whether to jump, go right or left or rush down again."

—George "Duffy" Lewis, in an interview with John Gillooly of the *Boston Record-American*

Duffy Lewis

19 Duffy's Cliff

When Fenway Park opened in 1912, a 25-foot wall was built in left field to prevent fans from gaining free entrance to the game by scaling the fence. It also blocked the view from rooftops across Lansdowne Street. A 10-foot embankment was installed at the base of the wall to allow standing-room crowds to see over one another. The slope became known as "Duffy's Cliff" from George "Duffy" Lewis' mastery of climbing it to play fly balls hit deep to left.

20 Harry Hooper

Only one player was a part of the four world championship teams the Red Sox fielded from 1912 through 1918 and that was Harry Hooper. A member of what has been described as the best outfield of the "Dead Ball Era" with Tris Speaker and Duffy Lewis, Hooper was a spectacular defensive outfielder. He was also a consistent leadoff hitter who still leads the Red Sox in triples (130) and stolen bases (300). Despite not being known for his power, in 1915 Hooper became the first player to hit two home runs in a World Series game, versus the Philadelphia Phillies. He was inducted into the Baseball Hall of Fame in 1971.

21 Tris Speaker

The greatest center fielder ever? It's hard to argue otherwise. Speaker holds the all-time baseball record for putouts and assists by an outfielder. He preferred to play shallow, turning balls that would normally fall for base hits into outs, as well as chasing down longer drives hit over his head that others would never catch up to. Playing as shallow as he did, essentially becoming a fifth infielder, "Spoke" was able to turn several unassisted double plays, including the only one recorded by an outfielder in World Series history, in 1912. With Duffy Lewis and Harry Hooper, Speaker anchored the best outfield of the "Dead Ball Era."

His athleticism carried over to the plate as well. Speaker batted .337 in his nine seasons with the Sox, and posted a .344 average for his entire career, tying him with Ted Williams. In addition to recording the unassisted double play in the 1912 World Series, Speaker singled in the tying run in the bottom of the 10th inning of the final game, and the Red Sox went on to win 3–2. He also holds the major league record for doubles with 792.

"I learned early that I could save more games by cutting off some of those singles than I could lose by having an occasional extra base hit go over my head."

—Tris Speaker

Tris Speaker

22 Through the Years

Since 1901, fans have been streaming through the gates of first Huntington Avenue Grounds and, later, Fenway Park. Generation upon generation have filled the seats and shared the joy of a day at the ballpark. Fathers and sons, mothers and daughters, grandparents and grandkids, aunts, uncles, nieces, and nephews, friends and neighbors have all formed a collective soul that is as much a part of the Red Sox as Fenway Park and the players themselves.

23 Wooden Seats

Fenway Park is the only major league stadium to still have wooden seats. While many of the seats in the park have been updated to newer, wider, and more comfortable versions, the wooden seats in the grandstand date to the early years of the park and measure a meager 15 inches across.

"New England's parlor, a region's nightclub, and the Olde Towne Team's hearth. To generations of Americans, going to Fenway Park has been like coming home."

—Curt Smith, *Our House: A Tribute to Fenway Park*

President Woodrow Wilson

24 0.96

Dutch Leonard's 1914 season ERA is still the major league record.

25 Joe Lannin

Lannin bought the team before the start of the 1914 season and made signing Tris Speaker to a new contract his first priority. Despite intense competition for players from the upstart Federal League, Lannin was able to fill his roster with loads of talent. In addition to Speaker, he signed Babe Ruth and Ernie Shore in the summer of 1914, and the Red Sox went on to win back-to-back World Series titles in 1915 and 1916.

26 Welcome Mr. President

Woodrow Wilson became the first president to attend a World Series game when he accompanied his fiancée, Edith Galt, to the second game of the 1915 Series between the Red Sox and the Philadelphia Phillies, a 2–1 Sox victory.

33

27 The Third World Championship, 1915

Boston won four straight games versus the Philadelphia Phillies after dropping the opener of the 1915 World Series. In a Game 3 victory, Dutch Leonard retired 20 straight Philadelphia hitters, and Harry Hooper provided the finishing touch in the finale with his game-winning home run. Red Sox pitching was the difference, as Boston's staff held the Phillies to an anemic .182 batting average.

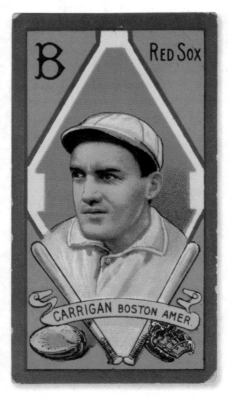

28 Bill Carrigan

Nicknamed "Rough" for his toughness in the field during his playing days, Carrigan was noted for his expert handling of pitchers while catching for the Red Sox. A prominent figure in Babe Ruth's development, Carrigan managed the Red Sox to World Series titles in 1915 and 1916.

"To motivate his pitchers [Carrigan] refused to name his starters for crucial games in advance. Then, on the day of the game, he'd stand before the entire team and ask, 'Who wants the ball?'"

—Glenn Stout and Richard A. Johnson, *Red Sox Century*

Bill Carrigan

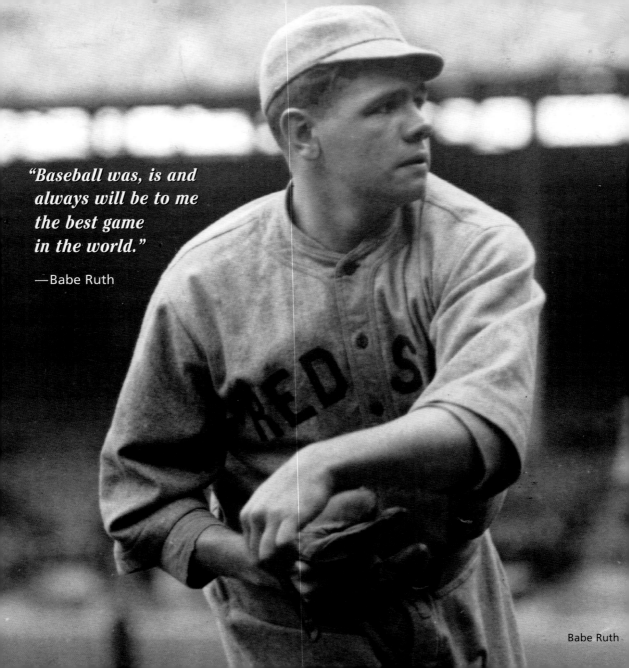

"*Baseball was, is and always will be to me the best game in the world.*"

—Babe Ruth

Babe Ruth

29 Babe Ruth

George Herman "Babe" Ruth, the greatest to ever play the game, got his major league start with the Red Sox. Sold to Boston along with Ernie Shore and Ben Egan in 1914 by the minor league Baltimore Orioles, Ruth quickly became a force on the mound and at the plate. He joined the Red Sox on July 11, 1914, and promptly pitched them to a victory over the Cleveland Indians in his first major league appearance. In his second game, versus New York, he banged out his first hit and scored his first run.

In 1916, Ruth beat Hall of Famer Walter Johnson four times in head-to-head pitching matchups, posting 23 wins for the season and a league-leading 1.75 ERA. He won his first World Series start versus the Brooklyn Dodgers in 1916, and went on to pitch 29 2/3 consecutive scoreless innings in World Series games, a record that was unmatched until 1961.

The Babe's career numbers in Boston include an 89–46 won-lost record, a .308 batting average, and 49 home runs in 5 1/2 seasons. He led the team to World Series titles in 1915, 1916 and 1918.

His sale to the Yankees in 1919, coupled with a severe decline in the quality of Red Sox teams in the subsequent years, became the source of "the curse" that haunted the Red Sox until their 2004 world championship.

30 Two in a Row, the 1916 World Champions

The 1916 World Series featured the Red Sox and the Brooklyn Dodgers, two teams built around pitching and defense. In Babe Ruth's first start in a World Series game, Boston won Game 2, 2–1, in 14 innings. The Red Sox went on to win their second consecutive world championship in five games, while beating Hall of Fame pitcher Rube Marquand twice. Boston became the third team in history to win two World Series in a row.

31 Harry Frazee

A self-made millionaire who had built his fortune in the theater, Frazee purchased the Red Sox from Joe Lannin in November of 1916 and stocked the roster with new talent that teamed with the remaining stars from the 1916 champions. Frazee's Red Sox went on to win their fifth World Series title in 1918.

Despised by countless fans for selling Babe Ruth to the Yankees in December of 1919, Frazee was merely conducting business as usual for him. Ruth had twice left the team without permission, was thought to be a physical risk with bad knees and a weight problem, and created unrest in the clubhouse by lobbying for the ouster of manager Ed Barrow. Frazee, who was crucified by the press in the ensuing years, simply did what he thought was best for his team. At the time, no one could have predicted the staggering success Ruth would achieve in his subsequent years with the Yankees.

"A team of players working harmoniously together is always preferred to that possessing one star who hugs the limelight all to himself. And that is what I'm after."

—Harry Frazee, from a statement regarding the sale of Babe Ruth, *Red Sox Century*, by Glenn Stout and Richard A. Johnson

39

32 The Babe and Ernie Show

On June 23, 1917, Babe Ruth and Ernie Shore combined to pitch what baseball recorded as a perfect game. Ruth actually walked the first batter, Ray Morgan, but was ejected for arguing with the umpire. Ernie Shore came on in relief, having not had time to warm up. Morgan was thrown out as he attempted to steal second, and Shore went on to retire the next 26 batters in a row.

33 One for the Thumb, 1918

Babe Ruth and the Boston Red Sox won their fifth World Series in 1918, defeating the Chicago Cubs 4 games to 2. Ruth tossed a shutout to open the Series and later extended his scoreless streak to 29 2/3 innings. But it was George Whiteman who was the real hero of the Series with his clutch hitting and sparkling fielding. His diving catch of a sinking liner in the eighth inning of Game 6 was, at the time, called the greatest catch in the history of the World Series.

"1918. Any real baseball fan knows the significance of that date. That was the last year the Boston Red Sox won the World Series… They've been trying to do it again ever since."

—Glenn Stout and Richard A. Johnson, *Red Sox Century*

Babe Ruth and Ernie Shore

34 The Curse

In December 1919, a year after Boston had won its fifth World Series, Red Sox owner Harry Frazee sold a disenchanted Babe Ruth to the Yankees. While the team's management agreed with the move, fans and reporters weren't happy. They loved Ruth for his talent and charisma, ignoring or not knowing of the problems he created in the clubhouse. Ruth and the Yankees soared to the top of the baseball world, where they've reigned for most of the past eight decades, while the Red Sox fell to the depths of mediocrity and ineptitude for years before finally winning another American League pennant. Over the next 85 years the Sox managed just four World Series appearances and each ended in a Game 7 loss. Fans and writers alike blamed this fate on "the curse of the Bambino," but it seems more a result of bad management, poor decisions, untimely mistakes, and unlucky breaks than any supernatural force. Finally, in 2004, the Red Sox put an end to the curse by defeating the Yankees in the ALCS and then sweeping the Cardinals for their first World Series title in 86 years.

"I don't believe in curses. Wake up the damn Bambino, maybe I'll drill him."

—Pedro Martinez

43

35 The Olde Towne

The city of Boston is one of the most beautiful and historic in all of America. Since the days of the American Revolution, the Olde Towne has been a center of culture, education, and business and Red Sox baseball has been a part of that for more than 100 years.

36 B is for Beloved

The crimson B that adorns the navy blue caps of the Red Sox is instantly recognizable to baseball fans everywhere. It is worn as a badge of honor by Red Sox fans displaying their devotion to their beloved team.

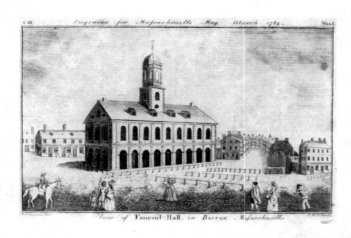

View of Faneuil Hall, in Boston, Massachusetts.

37 The Rivalry

It has to be the biggest, brightest, most heated rivalry in all of sports. Yanks versus Red Sox—those words change any ordinary baseball game into an epic struggle of titanic proportions. The rivalry dates back to 1903, the Yankees' first season. Boston had been America's center of culture and commerce, but New York's explosive growth was making it the preeminent city in America and the world. When the two teams first met on May 7, 1903, the Red Sox proved victorious, 6–2. Boston would continue to dominate the rivalry for some time, going on to win their first World Series title that year, and four more by 1918.

From 1919 through 2003, New York owned the rivalry, winning just about every game of significance between the two teams, as well as 26 world championships. The Red Sox finally struck a crushing blow of their own in 2004 by defeating the Yankees in the ALCS after trailing 3-games-to-none, and just three outs from a sweep in Game 4. Coupled with the Yankees' dramatic extra-inning victory in Game 7 of the 2003 ALCS, the rivalry has become more intense than ever. Only another World Series title is sweeter to Red Sox fans than beating the Yanks on any given day.

"It's white hot. It's a rivalry on the field, it's a rivalry in the press, it's a rivalry in the front office, it's a rivalry among the fan base. It's as good and intense a rivalry as any you could have."

—Larry Lucchino, Red Sox president, *Red Sox vs. Yankees, the Great Rivalry*

At left, Jason Varitek and Alex Rodriguez are separated by umpire Bruce Froemming

Tom Yawkey with wife, Jean

38 Tom Yawkey

Yawkey, who was the adopted son of his uncle William Yawkey, onetime owner of the Detroit Tigers, purchased the Red Sox in 1933 from a disenchanted Bob Quinn and hired former Philadelphia A's star Eddie Collins as vice president and general manager. Yawkey's deep pockets carried Boston's team through the end of the Depression as he renovated Fenway Park and acquired player after player in an attempt to win a world championship with the Red Sox.

Unfortunately for Boston and Yawkey, he didn't have the kind of success expected with his transactions. In his 44-year ownership of the franchise, the Sox won three pennants and lost the World Series in seven games, each time. Despite never winning the world championship he so coveted, Yawkey brought new respectability to the franchise with players like Ted Williams and Carl Yastrzemski and once again made Boston the best baseball town in America. In 1976, the city of Boston renamed Jersey Street Yawkey Way, in honor of the longtime owner.

39 The Green Monster

When Fenway Park was renovated for the 1934 season, the entire park was painted "Dartmouth green." In left field stood a new wall, rebuilt to accommodate a new electronic scoreboard. Just 310 feet from home plate in the left-field corner, the 37-foot-high wall became the most notable feature of Fenway Park. In 1947, the ads that were fixtures on the old wall were painted over, giving rise to the name. Forever controversial because of how a game can turn on any ball hit its way, the Green Monster makes Fenway Fenway.

40 Red for Strikes and Green for Balls

The manual scoreboard in the left-field wall is still operable with red and green lights to signal strikes, balls, and outs, and signs weighing 3 pounds to indicate runs. A room behind the scoreboard features walls covered with the signatures of many of the Red Sox players. The scoreboard operators have very few modern amenities, but one is an Internet connection, which allows them to post updated scores from around the league in a timely fashion.

"It is impossible to overstate what the Wall means to Fenway. It has changed the way the Red Sox play baseball, sometimes saving them, but more often killing them."

—Dan Shaughnessy, *Fenway, A Biography in Words and Pictures*

41 47,627

Fenway Park currently has a seating capacity of 33,871, but 47,627 fans came to watch the Red Sox battle the Yankees on September 22, 1935, in a doubleheader.

42 Joe Cronin

Purchased from the Washington Senators by new owner Tom Yawkey in 1934 for $250,000, Cronin batted over .300 seven times in 11 seasons with the Sox. He hit a career-high 24 home runs in 1940 and drove in 111 runs. He is ninth on Boston's all-time RBI list with 737. Cronin was also the first player to ever hit a pinch-hit home run from opposite sides of the plate in a doubleheader (one in each game). He managed the Red Sox for 13 seasons, accumulating 1,071 wins and leading the Sox to an American League pennant in 1946, their first since winning the 1918 World Series. His number, 4, is retired alongside the numbers of Bobby Doerr, Ted Williams, Carl Yastrzemski, and Carlton Fisk.

Joe Cronin

53

43 Lefty Grove

One of owner Tom Yawkey's major acquisitions in an attempt to buy a world championship for the Red Sox, Grove had already led the American League in strikeouts for seven consecutive years and posted a 31–4 record in 1931 when he was purchased from the Philadelphia Athletics in 1934. Despite playing for the Sox in the latter part of his career, Grove still managed to win 105 games over eight seasons, including 20 in 1935, capping his career with his 300th win in 1941, a 10–6 victory over Cleveland. Ted Williams considered Grove to be one of the best pitchers in baseball history. Grove was elected to the Baseball Hall of Fame in 1947.

44 Tickets to the Game

Nowhere in America are tickets to a game more cherished than in Boston's Fenway Park. The small venue with its long and rich history makes a ticket a precious commodity, difficult to obtain just about any time, but darn near impossible to get when the Sox are in contention. Legend has it that a fan who now lives in Thailand continues to purchase season tickets to guarantee himself seats for the World Series if the Red Sox make it that far.

Lefty Grove

Jimmie Foxx

45 Jimmie Foxx

"Double X," as he was commonly known, set the all-time Red Sox record for home runs in a season when he hit 50 in 1938. David Ortiz broke Foxx's 68-year-old record in 2006 when he hit 54. That year, Foxx won his third league MVP award, adding 175 RBI (also a team record) and batting .349. "The Beast," as he was also known, followed that remarkable season by hitting .360 in 1939 with 35 home runs and 105 RBI in just 124 games. In seven seasons with the Sox, Foxx totaled 222 home runs, 788 RBI, and compiled a .320 batting average. "The most liked man in baseball" became the second player in history to reach 500 career home runs when he slugged his 36th and last of the season in 1940. He is a member of the Baseball Hall of Fame and considered one of the best first basemen to ever play the game.

46 Sunshine

Helen Robinson was the switchboard operator for the Red Sox for 60 years. Beloved by the team and known throughout baseball, "Sunshine," as she was called by Ted Williams, never missed a day at work, arriving promptly at nine and staying an hour after every home game to field any last-minute calls. When many of the Red Sox players left to serve in the military during World War II and Korea, Helen knitted sweaters for each of them. She remained a part of the Red Sox family until her death in October 2001.

"Jimmie Foxx could hit me at midnight with the lights out."

—Lefty Gomez

47 Ted Williams

Fiery, passionate, and outspoken, Williams wanted to be known as "the greatest hitter who ever lived." He was tireless in his study and practice of hitting, and his quick wrists, keen eye, and discipline made him one of the very best to ever play the game.

The greatest Red Sox hitter ever spent his entire career in Boston, amassing a team record 521 home runs, a .344 career batting average, and 1,839 RBI, second only to Carl Yastrzemski's 1,844, despite missing all or part of five seasons while serving in the military. "The Kid" joined the Red Sox in 1939 at the age of 20, hitting .327 with 31 home runs and 145 RBI in his rookie season. Two years later, in 1941, the "Splendid Splinter" became the last major leaguer to hit over .400 in a season when he finished 1941 with a .406 average, including a now immortal 6-for-8 performance in a doubleheader on the last day of the season.

"Teddy Ballgame" finished his career with six batting titles, two Triple Crowns, and two MVP awards, including 1946, when he made his only appearance in the World Series. On September 28, 1960, he homered off Baltimore's Jack Fisher in the final at bat of his career. His number, 9, has been retired by the Red Sox.

"Trying to get a fastball by him was like trying to get a sunbeam by a rooster."

—Bob Feller

Ted Williams

48 Williamsburg

In 1940, team management decided to make it easier for Ted Williams to hit home runs by moving the bullpens from foul territory to right field in front of the bleachers. This brought the right-field fence in by some 22 feet, turning many of Williams', (and others') long outs into homers. The bullpen area has come to be known as "Williamsburg."

49 Section 42, Row 37, Seat 21

Painted red in a sea of green, this seat, which is more than 30 rows beyond the bullpen in right field, marks the point where the longest measurable home run ever hit in Fenway landed, sort of. Measured at 502 feet, Ted Williams' June 9, 1946 smash bounced off the straw hat–covered head of Joseph Boucher who later said, "They say it bounced a dozen rows higher, but after it hit my head, I was no longer interested." Boucher, an engineer from Albany, New York, often took in Red Sox games when he was in town on business and remained a devoted fan after the incident.

50 My Guys

Ted Williams remained close friends throughout his life with fellow players Bobby Doerr, Johnny Pesky, and Dom DiMaggio. He called the group "my guys." All four were born at the end of World War I, and Williams, Doerr, and DiMaggio played in the Pacific Coast League together before moving on to the majors. Pesky was a clubhouse attendant in Portland, Oregon, at the time, responsible for shining the visiting players' shoes, and got to know each of the others there before making his way to Boston as well.

51 The Little Professor

Hall of Famer Joe DiMaggio's brother Dom played 10-plus seasons with the Red Sox and batted .298 for his career. Along with Tris Speaker and Fred Lynn, "the Little Professor" was one of the best center fielders ever to play in Fenway, twice leading the league in runs scored. He also put together a Red Sox record 34-game hitting streak in 1949.

"For many years, the glue that held them together as friends was Williams; someone that great, one of the very best ever at what they all did, had rare peer power."

—David Halberstam, *The Teammates*

Johnny Pesky, Dom DiMagg[io],
Bobby Doerr, manager Stev[e]
O'Neil, and Ted Williams

Bobby Doerr and
Johnny Pesk

52 Bobby Doerr

The best second baseman in the history of the Red Sox, and one of the best in all of baseball, Doerr established the record for home runs hit by a Boston second baseman with 223. He twice hit 27 in a season, a team record that has stood for over 50 years. He's fifth on Boston's all-time RBI list with 1,247. In his only World Series appearance in 1946, Doerr hit safely in all seven games, batting .409 for the Series. Hitting wasn't his only talent, however. Doerr was as smooth in the field as he was strong at the plate, twice setting American League records for games and chances in the field without an error, including a streak of 73 games and 414 chances in 1948. One of the Red Sox' all-time greats, Doerr had his number, 1, retired in 1988.

53 Johnny Pesky

Pesky spent eight seasons playing for the Red Sox, but never really left. Playing shortstop for some of the strongest teams ever fielded in Boston, Pesky led the league in hits his first three seasons, despite missing three years while he was in the service between his first and second seasons. He hit over .300 six times and his on-base percentage topped .400 three consecutive years from 1949 to 1951. Given the nickname "Needlenose" by his teammates, Pesky has continued to work in the Red Sox organization for nearly all of the past 60 years.

54 Pesky's Pole

Sox pitcher Mel Parnell dubbed the right-field foul pole in Fenway "Pesky's Pole" after shortstop Johnny Pesky won a game with a homer that landed just beyond the marker—one of only six homers Pesky hit at Fenway during his career.

55 Red, White, and Blue

Between 1942 and 1945, 22 Boston players exchanged their Red Sox uniforms for those of the military to serve America during World War II. Those players put in a combined 53 years of service. All but one player from the starting lineup of the 1946 American League pennant winners served.

56 Elizabeth Dooley

Daughter of John Dooley, one of the leaders of the Royal Rooters, Dooley held front-row season tickets to the Red Sox for 55 years. She became fast friends with many players, including Ted Williams, and considered the Sox her "extended family," as they did her.

"Forever, she's the greatest Red Sox fan there'll ever be. She is a sweet thing."

—Ted Williams, on Elizabeth Dooley, from *At Fenway, Dispatches Red Sox Nation,* by Dan Shaughnessy

57 The CITGO Sign

Dominating the Boston skyline over the Green Monster in left field is the 60 x 60–foot neon CITGO sign. Originally installed in 1940, and replaced in 1965, the sign is one of Boston's most recognizable landmarks. Fans know they're minutes from Fenway Park when they find themselves in the shadow of the sign perched high above Boston's Kenmore Square.

Roy Partee slides past
catcher Joe Garagiola as
Johnny Pesky looks on

58 1946

With Dom DiMaggio leading off, followed by Johnny Pesky, Ted Williams, and Bobby Doerr, and Tex Hughson on the mound, the 1946 Red Sox opened the season loaded with talent and promise. They got off to a great start, winning 15 in a row in late April and early May, and by mid-season had the pennant all but wrapped up. The Sox clinched the pennant on, of all days, Friday, September 13 as Williams and company went on to finish the regular season 104–50, 12 games ahead of the second-place Detroit and 17 games in front of Joe DiMaggio's Yankees. Boasting a remarkable 60–16 record at Fenway Park, the Red Sox prepped for the World Series with a couple of exhibition games against American League all-stars while awaiting the outcome of a 3-game playoff between the St. Louis Cardinals and the Brooklyn Dodgers. Both Williams and DiMaggio were injured in the first exhibition and Williams played his only World Series with a severely bruised elbow. The Sox won the opener and led the Series 3 games to 2, but the Cardinals came back to take the last two, winning Game 7 on Enos Slaughter's "Mad Dash" in the bottom of the eighth.

59 The Jimmy Fund

When the National League Boston Braves relocated to Milwaukee just prior to the start of the 1953 season, Braves owner Lou Perini asked Red Sox owner Tom Yawkey to take over his local children's cancer charity, the Jimmy Fund, part of the Dana-Farber Cancer Institute in Boston. The bond between the two organizations has deepened over the years as the Red Sox have helped raise millions of dollars in support of their favorite charity. Jimmy Fund collection boxes are mounted on Fenway's superstructure throughout the park.

60 Mel Parnell

Considered by many as the best left-handed pitcher in Red Sox history, Parnell is third in wins for the Red Sox with 123, behind only Roger Clemens and Cy Young. From 1949 to 1953 Parnell won at least 18 games four times, including a remarkable 25–7 record in 1949. In July of 1956 Parnell put an exclamation point on his Red Sox career by pitching a no-hitter against the White Sox—the first by a Boston pitcher since 1923.

61 This Isn't Football

The Red Sox put up 17 runs in the seventh inning of the June 18, 1953, game versus the Detroit Tigers—a number more commonly seen on a football scoreboard. Boston sent 23 batters to the plate, collecting 14 hits and six walks. Gene Stephens led the way with three hits in the inning, all of which was accomplished without Ted Williams, who was off fighting in the Korean War.

This statue outside Fenway Park depicts Ted Williams placing his Red Sox cap on the head of a young Jimmy Fund cancer patient.

Fenway

A BIOGRAPHY
IN WORDS AND PICTURES

DAN SH

FOREWORD B

ONE HUNDRED YEARS OF RED SOX BASEBALL

RED SOX
C E N T U R Y

INCLUDING ESSAYS BY
PETER GAMMONS
CHARLES P. PIERCE
BILL LITTLEFIELD
DAN SHAUGHNESSY
TIM HORGAN
HOWARD BRYANT
LUKE SALISBURY
ELIZABETH DOOLEY

GLENN STOUT AND RICHARD A. JOHNSON

THE
TEAMMATES

A Portrait of a Friendship

VID HALBERSTAM

62 Voices of a Nation

In 1984, former Red Sox announcer Curt Gowdy was inducted into the writers and broadcasters wing of the Baseball Hall of Fame. One of the most recognizable voices in all of baseball, Gowdy joined the Boston broadcast team in 1951 and was a fixture until 1966, when he left to become the NBC *Game of the Week* announcer. He is part of a long list of esteemed men who have been known as the "Voice of the Red Sox," including Fred Hoey, Tom Hussey, Ned Martin, Ken Coleman, and Sean McDonough.

Since 1969, Peter Gammons' writing has resonated with a new generation of baseball fans in New England. His words provide a literary voice for Red Sox Nation.

63 Well Red

Over the years, many great books have been written about the Red Sox. Some of the best include:

My Turn at Bat: The Story of My Life, by Ted Williams with John Underwood
Fenway: A Biography in Words and Pictures, by Dan Shaughnessy and Stan Grossfeld
Red Sox Century, by Glenn Stout and Richard A. Johnson
Impossible Dreams: A Red Sox Collection, by Glenn Stout
The Teammates, by David Halberstam

64 The Monster

Red Sox pitcher Dick Radatz recorded 47 strikeouts while allowing only one hit in 63 at bats to Yankee slugger Mickey Mantle, earning him Mantle's utmost respect and the nickname "the Monster."

65 Dick O'Connell

Tom Yawkey's general manager from 1965 to 1977, O'Connell helped resurrect a stagnant and slumbering franchise by hiring Dick Williams to manage the team in 1967 and signing players like Carlton Fisk, Jim Rice, and Fred Lynn. The team, a bottom-dweller for several years running, surged to the World Series in 1967 and 1975.

66 Dick Williams

In one of the most incredible single-season performances by a manager in the history of the game, Williams took a nearly dead Boston franchise and brought it back from the brink in 1967, leading the Red Sox on their "Impossible Dream." His leadership reenergized a downtrodden franchise that to this day continues to be one of the best in baseball.

"He's the greatest relief pitcher I've ever seen."

—Yankee manager Ralph Houk, on Dick Radatz

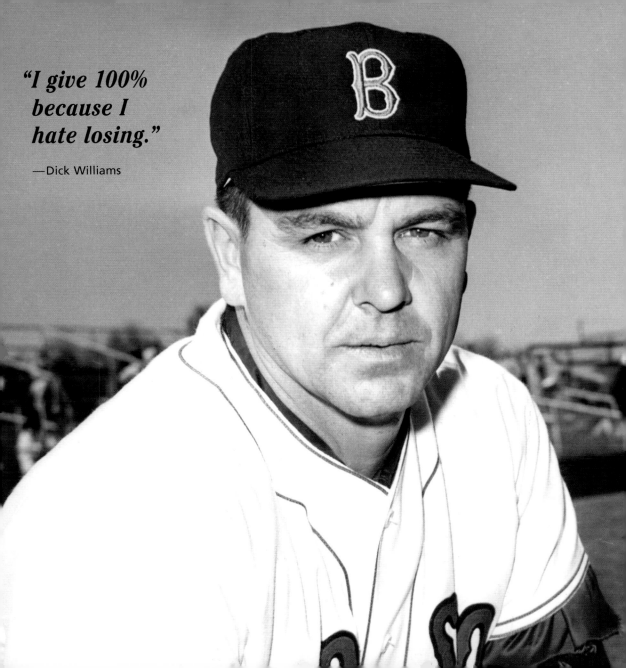

"I give 100% because I hate losing."

—Dick Williams

67 The Impossible Dream

After losing 100 games in 1965, 90 more in 1966, and finishing ninth both seasons, there was little hope when the 1967 season began. But general manager Dick O'Connell had hired the fiery Dick Williams as the new manager of the Red Sox, and Williams proved to be the taskmaster the team needed to reverse its fortunes.

Rookie Billy Rohr kick-started the remarkable season by pitching a 1-hit shutout in the Yankees' home opener. Rohr was one pitch away from posterity when Elston Howard singled with two outs and a full count in the ninth inning. The victory served notice that the 1967 season would be a far cry from the failures of recent years.

By the All-Star break, no team had separated itself from the pack and the pennant was up for grabs. On August 18, Tony Conigliaro was horribly injured when he was hit in the face by a wild pitch, but the Red Sox went on to win the game and sweep four straight from the Angels. A few days later, for the first time in nearly 20 years, Boston found itself in first place in August. But as the race to the pennant entered its final month, four teams, the Sox, Twins, Tigers, and White Sox, were in a virtual dead heat. That's when Carl Yastrzemski put the Sox on his back and carried them to the pennant. Over the final 12 games he batted .523 and made several spectacular plays in the field as the Sox won eight of those games, including the last two in a head-to-head matchup with the Twins that determined the pennant winner.

The dream ended in Game 7 of the World Series versus the St. Louis Cardinals when Jim Lonborg finally ran out of gas, and Bob Gibson shut the Sox down one more time to give the Cardinals the world championship. The Red Sox may have lost the World Series, but they had won back their fans, and reenergized the town of Boston and its love for baseball.

68 Carl Yastrzemski

In 1961, rookie Carl "Yaz" Yastrzemski replaced the legendary Ted Williams in left field. Playing in the shadow of the Green Monster, Yaz filled Williams' shoes better than anyone expected. Throughout his career he played the game with passion and dignity. In 1967, one year after the Sox finished ninth in the American League, 26 games out of first place, Yaz carried the Red Sox to the World Series with an MVP and Triple Crown performance that included a .326 batting average, 44 home runs, and 121 RBI. With a 4-for-4 performance in the last game of the regular season, and 23 for his last 44, he was the difference in giving the Sox the pennant by one game over Detroit and Minnesota in a season that became known as the "Impossible Dream."

Yaz played 3,308 games for the Red Sox in his 23-year career, an American League record. He holds the team record for RBI with 1,844, is second in homers with 452, and won the AL batting title three times. His number, 8, is one of five numbers retired by the Red Sox.

"Yaz wore number eight. I had noticed that, starting in 1975, Carl was taking catnaps in the trainer's room. With his uniform on. When laid on its side the number 8 resembles the symbol for infinity. That symbol was recharging Yaz's batteries. If he had just worn his uniform while he slept at night, I am convinced he could have played forever."

—Bill Lee, *The Wrong Stuff*

Ted Williams and Carl Yastrzemski

Tony Conigliaro

69 Rico Petrocelli

On October 1, 1967, Petrocelli caught the final out of the game on the last day of the season as Boston defeated Minnesota and clinched the pennant in their "Impossible Dream" season. A fixture for 12 years playing shortstop and later third base for the Sox, Petrocelli hit 40 home runs in 1969, then a league record for shortstops. He also homered twice in Game 6 of the 1967 World Series and was the starting shortstop on two All-Star teams.

70 Tony Conigliaro

A local boy from Swampscott, Massachusetts, Conigliaro joined the Red Sox in 1964 at the age of 19. He hit 24 homers in his rookie season that ended prematurely in August after he broke his arm. "Tony C" returned in 1965 to hit 32 home runs, becoming the youngest player ever to lead the league in that category. An instant hero with his home run power and movie star looks, Conigliaro teamed with Carl Yastrzemski, Rico Petrocelli, Jim Lonborg, and the rest of the 1967 Sox in their quest for the "Impossible Dream." In one of the most horrifying incidents in baseball history, Tony C's season, and very nearly his life, came to an abrupt end when he was hit just under his left eye by a fastball that got away from California pitcher Jack Hamilton. A fractured cheekbone, dislocated jaw, and damaged retina in his left eye forced Conigliaro to sit out the 1968 season as well, but he returned to hit 20 homers in 1969, winning the "Comeback Player of the Year" award, and followed that effort with 36 round-trippers and 116 RBI in 1970.

71 The Spaceman

Bill Lee always seemed to have a unique perspective on baseball and the world in general. This earned him the moniker "the Spaceman." When he first got a look at the Green Monster he asked if "they leave it there during games." He nicknamed his manager Don Zimmer "the gerbil," and once called All-Star teammate Carl Yastrzemski "the worst dresser in organized baseball." Always outspoken, Lee wanted to outlaw mascots, Astroturf, and the designated hitter, but bring back nickel beer at the ballpark. When he wasn't philosophizing, he managed to find time to pitch for 10 years with the Red Sox, putting together three consecutive 17-win seasons from 1973 to 1975.

72 The All-Name Team

Through the years, the Red Sox roster has included many colorful names, such as: Asby Asbjornson, Matt Batts, Red Bluhm, Dennis "Oil Can" Boyd, King Brady, Hick Cady, Esty Chancy, Hoot Evers, Homer Ezzell, Happy Foreman, Fabian Gaffke, Skinny Graham, Pumpsie Green, Turkey Gross, Piano Legs Hickman, Baby Doll Jacobson, Sad Sam Jones, Candy LaChance, Heinie Manush, Johnny Peacock, Rip Repulski, Pop Rising, Red Ruffing, Biff Schlitzer, Ossee Schreckengost, Heathcliff Slocumb, Riverboat Smith, Dizzy Trout, Rabbit Warstler, Pinky Woods, and at least four guys named Chick.

"*Do you realize that even as we sit here, we are hurtling through space at a tremendous rate of speed? Think about it. Our world is just a hanging curveball.*"

—Bill Lee

73 Carlton Fisk

Probably best remembered for his dramatic game-winning home run in the 12th inning of Game 6 of the 1975 World Series, Fisk owns the record for longevity by a major league catcher with 24 seasons behind the plate. "Pudge" caught 2,226 games, more than any other catcher in major league history, and hit 351 of his 376 career home runs as a catcher — a record that lasted until 2004 when it was broken by the Mets' Mike Piazza. Fisk played 10 seasons with the Red Sox, including his rookie campaign in 1972 when he batted .293, hit 22 home runs, delivered nine triples, and won the Rookie of the Year award. A team leader from the start of his career, Pudge played with a fire and intelligence that infused his team with a winning spirit. Inducted into the Baseball Hall of Fame, his number, 27, was retired by the Red Sox in 2000.

74 1, 4, 8, 9, and 27

These five numbers, belonging to Bobby Doerr, Joe Cronin, Carl Yastrzemski, Ted Williams, and Carlton Fisk, respectively, are the only numbers retired by the Red Sox. Jackie Robinson's number, 42, retired by Major League Baseball, hangs with them in right field.

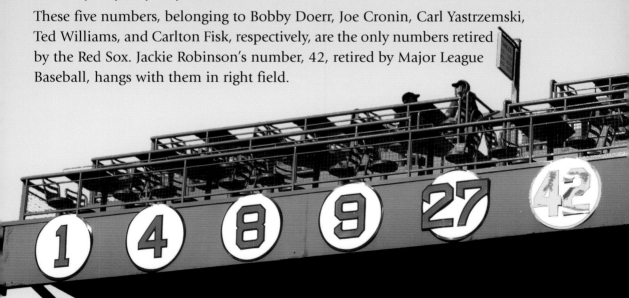

75 Game 6, 1975

Trailing the Cincinnati Reds 3 games to 2 in 1975 World Series, the Red Sox turned to veteran Luis Tiant to resurrect their World Series hopes. Boston opened an early 3–0 lead, but Cincinnati tied the game in the fifth inning, and then sent Tiant to the showers in the eighth, with Cincy leading 6–3.

With two on in the bottom of the eighth, Bernie Carbo, pinch-hitting for Roger Moret, drove the second pitch he saw into the center-field bleachers, tying the game and breathing new life into the Red Sox and their fans.

In the top of the 11th Dwight Evans saved the game for Boston by making a leaping catch at the fence of a drive off the bat of Joe Morgan, then turned and threw to first for an inning-ending double play.

With the game still tied in the bottom of the 12th, Carlton Fisk came to the plate. After taking ball one, Fisk lifted a long fly deep to left field. It curled perilously toward the stands in foul territory. Fisk implored the ball to stay fair, leaping and swinging his arms as he bounced down the first base line. The ball clanged off the foul pole in left, making it a fair ball, and a game-winning home run. Fenway erupted into joyful ecstasy as Game 6 took its place in baseball history books as one for the ages and Red Sox fans everywhere shared one glorious moment.

"And all of a sudden the ball was there, like the Mystic River Bridge suspended out in the black of morning."

—Peter Gammons,
in his story for the *Boston Globe*,
October 22, 1975

Jim Rice

76 Jim Rice

Rice and fellow rookie Fred Lynn, known as the "Gold Dust Twins," teamed up in 1975 to help the Red Sox to their second World Series appearance in eight years. Rice would miss the Fall Classic after breaking his hand just prior to the end of the season, but his offensive heroics were a key component in the Red Sox drive to the pennant. Had Rice not been injured, the Red Sox may very well have won their first world championship since 1918.

Continuing the tradition of great left fielders to play in the shadow of the Green Monster, Rice spent 16 seasons in Boston and stands third all-time in home runs and RBI, behind Ted Williams and Carl Yastrzemski. He won the American League MVP award in 1978 with 46 homers, 139 RBI, and a .315 batting average. Over the three-season span of 1977–79, he averaged 41 home runs and nearly 128 RBI per season.

77 Fred Lynn

Lynn played only six full seasons with the Red Sox, but he will always be remembered as one of their most exciting players. In 1975, teaming with fellow rookie Jim Rice, Lynn was an integral part of the Red Sox' title chase, slugging 21 home runs, and batting .331 with 105 RBI, becoming the first player ever to capture the Rookie of the Year and MVP awards in the same season. In center field he was a gritty and gifted performer, often risking injury to make a tough catch. In 1979 Lynn, who made six All-Star Game appearances, won the batting title with a .333 average.

78 Luis Tiant

"El Tiante" was rescued from the minor league scrap heap by the Red Sox in 1971. From 1972–76 Tiant was the ace of the Boston pitching staff, never winning fewer than 15 games, including posting an ERA of 1.91 in 1972 and striking out 206 batters in 272 innings pitched in 1973. A fan favorite with his signature Fu Manchu mustache and quirky, twirling windup, El Tiante led the Red Sox to two victories over the Reds in the 1975 World Series.

On game days at Fenway Park, Tiant can often be found roaming the stands, greeting fans, posing for photos, and signing autographs.

"When I'm in Boston, I always feel like I'm home. I almost cry, I feel so good."

—Luis Tiant

79 Dwight Evans

A gutsy performer who worked magic in the field with his glove and rifle arm, "Dewey" also produced with his bat. In his 20 years with the Sox, he hit 20 or more home runs in nine consecutive seasons and 11 of 12 years starting in 1978. He is fourth all-time in home runs and RBI for the Red Sox. Second behind Carl Yastrzemski in games played with the Sox, Evans also won eight Gold Gloves while presiding over Fenway's right field.

80 A Beer and a Dog

Nothing's better than a beer and a hot dog at the ballpark, and it doesn't get much better than a Fenway Frank and a cold brew. Fenway Franks are so popular they're even sold in supermarkets.

Food vendors also feature many selections unique to Fenway Park, including the El Tiante Cubano Sandwich, named for former Sox pitcher Luis Tiant, who runs the sandwich stand along Yawkey Way.

Legal Seafood Clam Chowder is another popular choice. Fans line up to get a cup of this world-famous New England–style clam chowder, which has been served at numerous presidential inaugurations. A perfect way to warm up on chilly game days in the spring and fall, the chowder is just as popular in the heat of summer.

Concessionaires serve "Monster Dogs," named in honor of the famed wall. These extra-large hot dogs weigh in at half a pound. Now that's a monster dog!

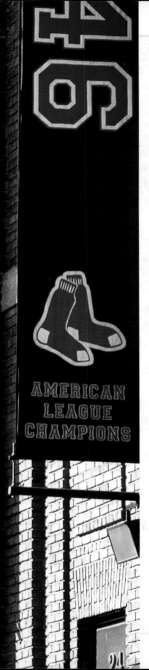

81 Yawkey Way

This street that fronts Fenway Park is closed to traffic before games to allow fans to comfortably stroll under the championship banners that hang off the ballpark's facade while they deliberate their choices of food and drink that line the way.

82 Wade Boggs

Boggs was methodical to a fault, and extremely super-stitious. Before every game, he ate chicken, took batting practice and ran sprints at precisely the same time, and always took the same number of ground balls in practice. Before each at bat, Boggs would draw the Hebrew symbol for life in the batter's box. His approach made him one of the greatest hitters ever to wear a Red Sox uniform. Boggs started his career in Boston by hitting .349 in 1982 and followed that by hitting over .350 five of the next six years. He strung together seven consecutive 200-hit seasons, and reached base safely in 80 percent of his games, a remarkable statistic. He holds the second highest career batting average in Red Sox history, .338, and is fifth in hits with 2,098. Boggs played in 12 consecutive All-Star games and anchored the Red Sox infield at third base for 11 years, including the 1986 American League pennant winners.

83 20 x 2

Roger Clemens fanned the Seattle Mariners'
Spike Owen and Phil Bradley in the ninth
inning of their April 29, 1986, game to tie
and break the all-time major league single-
game strikeout record of 19, held by Steve
Carlton, Tom Seaver, and Nolan Ryan.
Clemens repeated the feat 10 years later
when he struck out another 20 in the
fall of 1996 while pitching against the
Detroit Tigers.

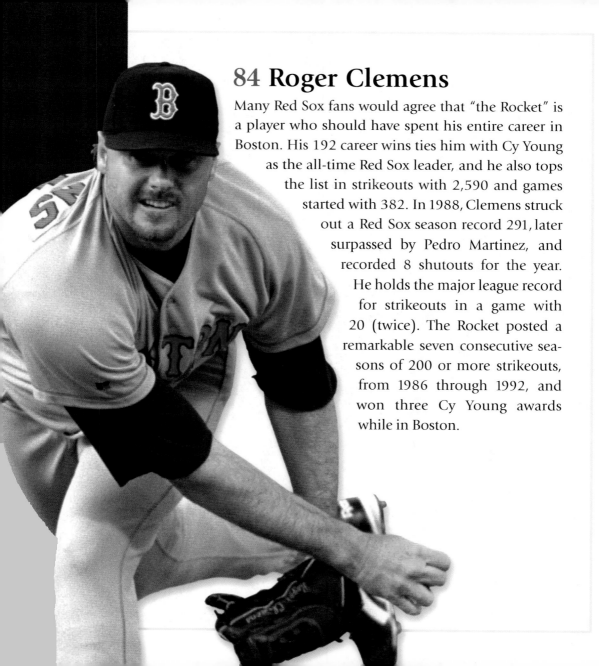

84 Roger Clemens

Many Red Sox fans would agree that "the Rocket" is a player who should have spent his entire career in Boston. His 192 career wins ties him with Cy Young as the all-time Red Sox leader, and he also tops the list in strikeouts with 2,590 and games started with 382. In 1988, Clemens struck out a Red Sox season record 291, later surpassed by Pedro Martinez, and recorded 8 shutouts for the year. He holds the major league record for strikeouts in a game with 20 (twice). The Rocket posted a remarkable seven consecutive seasons of 200 or more strikeouts, from 1986 through 1992, and won three Cy Young awards while in Boston.

85 Henderson's Heroics

October 12, 1986. Trailing the California Angels 5–4 with two outs in the ninth inning of Game 5 of the American League Championship Series, one strike away from an early exit from the play-offs, Dave Henderson turned on a Donnie Moore fastball and launched a 2-run home run into the left-field seats, giving the Red Sox a brief 6–5 lead. The Angels tied the game at 6 in the bottom of the ninth, but Henderson came through again in the 11th inning, with a sacrifice fly to center field that scored Don Baylor, giving the Red Sox a 7–6 victory. The Sox went on to win the series to earn a spot in the 1986 World Series versus the Mets.

"History does not wear a B on his cap."

—Glenn Stout and Richard A. Johnson, *Red Sox Century*

86 Game 6, 1986

One may ask why this woeful night in 1986 is a reason to love the Red Sox, but love is often felt most strongly in tragedy and loss. This game probably defines the Red Sox as much as any other single event in their history.

Up 3 games to 2 in the 1986 World Series, playing the Mets in Shea Stadium, Dave Henderson led off the 10th with a home run and Marty Barrett's single drove in Wade Boggs, who had doubled, to give Boston a 5–3 lead. Calvin Schiraldi got the first two outs in the bottom of the 10th inning, to put the Red Sox one out away from victory, but then Gary Carter and Kevin Mitchell singled. Schiraldi threw two strikes past Ray Knight and the Sox were one pitch from ending 68 years of misery. A fastball jammed Knight, but he fought it off and hit a broken-bat single to score Carter. Bob Stanley replaced Schiraldi, and after getting two strikes on Mookie Wilson the Red Sox were one strike away again. Wilson fouled off two pitches and then Stanley's next pitch got away from catcher Rich Gedman. Mitchell scored from third and Knight moved up to second. After fouling off two more pitches, Wilson squibbed a funky roller toward Bill Buckner at first. When Buckner misjudged the hop and let the ball bounce through his legs, Knight scored from second to win the game, and the Mets went on to win Game 7 and the Series.

Much has been made of Buckner's miscue, but it was a sequence of events that doomed the Red Sox and, for so long, served as a sort of microcosm of Boston's history of coming up just short. The roller coaster of emotions within this single game, and the pain and suffering this defeat brought on the team and its fans bonded forever those who endured it.

87 Mayday Malone

Sam Malone, the fictional character played by Ted Danson on the hit television show *Cheers*, was a bar owner and former relief pitcher for the Red Sox. The lovable "Mayday Malone" got his nickname from his tendency to give up long home runs.

88 Morgan Magic

In 1988, still playing with a hangover from the 1986 World Series debacle, the Red Sox fired manager John McNamara in mid-season and replaced him with Joe Morgan. The Red Sox went on to win 19 of their next 20 games to catch and pass the Yankees, sweeping a 3-game series in September, as they rolled to their second division title in three years.

Mike Greenwell

AMER

	1	2	3	4	5	6	7	8
CLEVE	1	1	0	0	0	4	0	0 0
BOSTON	2	5	3	5	5	3	0	3 2

BAT - BALL - STRIKE OUT

89 Mo, Mo, Mo

Mo Vaughn, the 1995 American League MVP, hit .330, homered 39 times, and drove in 126 runs in his MVP season, then followed that with 44 homers, 143 RBI, and a .326 batting average in 1996. He twice homered three times in one game for the Red Sox, once in 1996, and again in 1997, in a 10–4 victory over the New York Yankees. In seven-plus seasons with the Red Sox, Vaughn hit 230 home runs and batted .304.

90 Lighting It Up

On October 10, 1999, the Red Sox set a postseason record for runs scored in one game when they defeated Cleveland 23–7 in Game 4 of the American League Division Series. The onslaught included records for most hits (24), at bats (48), and total bases (44), and was spearheaded by Mike Stanley's five hits, John Valentin's seven RBI, and Jason Varitek's five runs scored.

91 Nomar Garciaparra

Named after his father, Ramon, who creatively reversed the spelling of his own name, Garciaparra has all the tools of a superstar. In every year through 2003 in which he played at least 135 games, Garciaparra hit over .300, including .357 in 1999 and .372 in 2000. In his 1997 Rookie of the Year season he slammed 30 home runs and fashioned a 30-game hitting streak. His 365 total bases broke Ted Williams' Red Sox rookie record of 344, as he became the first Red Sox player since Jackie Jensen in 1956 to reach double figures in doubles, triples, home runs, and steals. With extraordinary talent that extends to all aspects of the game, Garciaparra should be a lock for the Hall of Fame if he continues to produce numbers similar to those he put together in his eight and a half seasons in Boston.

"I cannot tell you how many times we've sat there in the dugout and gone, 'how the hell did he do that?' He never gets fooled, almost never breaks a bat. He couldn't care less about what a pitcher throws. He figures if it's a strike or anything close to it, he'll hit it."

—Lou Merloni

"This is what heaven must look like."

—Fred Pfannenstiehl, a lifelong Sox fan

92 Field of Dreams

In the wonderfully magical film *Field of Dreams*, based on the novel *Shoeless Joe* by W. P. Kinsella, Iowa farmer Ray Kinsella (played by Kevin Costner) and reclusive novelist Terrence Mann (played by James Earl Jones) visit Fenway Park while searching for answers as to why Kinsella has been prompted by a ghostly voice to build a ball field in his cornfield. During the game, the mysterious voice directs the two men to "go the distance" and images on the scoreboard help to persuade them to find "Moonlight" Graham, a player from long ago, as Kinsella's field becomes a place for players from baseball's past, including his own father, to once again play the game they love.

93 Keeping it Green

Current Fenway groundskeeper Dave Mellor and groundskeeper emeritus Joe Mooney have the never-ending job of maintaining Fenway Park's facilities and field, known for its lush, emerald green grass. The groundskeepers work from sun up to sundown, keeping Fenway as green as can be.

94 Mueller's Grand

Bill Mueller became the first player in major league history to hit grand slams from both sides of the plate in one game, on July 29, 2003, in a 14–7 victory over the Texas Rangers. He actually launched 3 home runs on the night, hitting a solo shot in the first inning, and drove in a total of 9 runs.

95 Rob Barry is Nuts

Fenway peanut vendor Rob Barry has perfected the art of tossing bags of peanuts long distances to hungry fans—so long in fact that he is the subject of a Trivial Pursuit question. Rob's secret: he tapes a small tack to his thumb that allows him to puncture the sealed peanut bags and squeeze out the excess air right before tossing them, making the package more compact and aerodynamic.

96 Monster Seats

For the 2003 season, the Red Sox added 275 seats atop the Green Monster. Lucky fans get to sit high above the playing field with a spectacular, if distant, view of the action and the rest of Fenway Park.

"I was just trying to drive some runs in. I was fortunate to get some balls up in the air and they carried out."

—Bill Mueller

Bill Mueller

97 Pedro Martinez

One of the most feared pitchers in baseball, Martinez baffles hitters by mixing a blazing fastball with a deadly split-finger fastball and curve, using incredible control to keep the opposing hitters off balance and guessing. Martinez joined the Red Sox in 1998 and led them to the ALCS in 1999, posting a 23–4 regular season record with an ERA of 2.07 and an incredible team record 313 strikeouts while winning the Cy Young Award. He followed his 1999 performance with another Cy Young year in 2000. And, in the defining moment of his career, Martinez helped end 86 years of frustration in Boston with his 7-inning, 3-hit performance in Game 3 of the 2004 World Series, a 4–1 Red Sox victory over the Cardinals.

"I've seen Nolan Ryan at his finest and Roger Clemens at his finest, and Martinez's control is better than either one."

—American League umpire Larry McCoy,
Detroit Free Press

98 Curt Schilling

He said he came to the Red Sox to help them win their first world championship since 1918 and, boy, did he ever deliver.

Schilling carried the Red Sox all of 2004. He led the major leagues in victories, posting a 21–6 record. His 3.26 ERA was second best in the American League, and he was third in the league in strikeouts with 203.

In the American League Divison Series, Schilling pitched the Red Sox to a Game 1 victory but re-injured an ailing right ankle late in the game. After the Sox completed a 3-game sweep of the Angels, Schilling tried to lead the Sox to victory in Game 1 of the American League Championship Series versus the Yankees, but the ruptured tendon in his ankle limited his ability to pitch effectively and the Yankees went on to win the first three games of the series. Following two extra-innings victories that kept the Red Sox in the series, team doctors performed an ingenious procedure in which they sutured the injured tendon to the skin to stabilize it, allowing Schilling to pitch seven innings of 4-hit ball in Game 6, as the Red Sox took a 4–2 victory. Putting the ghosts of the past to rest, the Sox went on to win Game 7 and complete an historic and unprecedented comeback against the archrival Yankees.

Then came the World Series. Prior to Game 2, Schilling underwent the painful procedure on his ankle for the second time in less than a week. He then went out and shut down the powerful Cardinals lineup on four hits over seven innings, allowing no earned runs. His heroic effort helped catapult the Red Sox to the team's first World Series title in 86 years. Schilling's performance was simply extraordinary, some say miraculous.

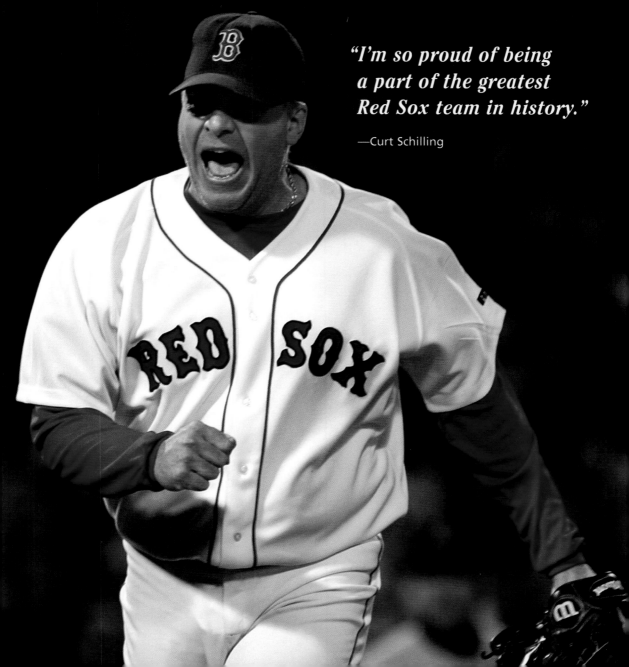

"I'm so proud of being a part of the greatest Red Sox team in history."

—Curt Schilling

99 Big Papi

No one has a flair for the dramatic like David Ortiz. No one delivers in the clutch like "Big Papi." Since 2004, when Ortiz led the Sox back from the brink against the Yankees in the ALCS, Big Papi has delivered more times than UPS, or so it seems. In just a few years, he has become a Red Sox legend and a Yankees nightmare. Papi's 54 home runs in 2006 broke Jimmie Foxx's all-time Red Sox record of 50, which had stood since 1938. And the hits just keep coming.

100 Keeping the Faith

One year after losing to the Yankees in Game 7 of the 2003 ALCS on Aaron Boone's 11th-inning walk-off home run, the Red Sox found themselves back in Yankee Stadium for another ALCS Game 7 showdown. The Sox had dropped the first three games of the series, including a 19–8 laugher at Fenway in Game 3. Three outs from being swept, Boston rallied against legendary Yankee closer Mariano Rivera, sending Game 4 into extra innings and winning on David Ortiz' 12th-inning homer. One night later, after once again rallying to tie the game against Rivera, Ortiz delivered another game-winning hit, this time a 14th inning single that scored Johnny Damon. The Series returned to New York for Game 6, where Curt Schilling pitched the Sox to a 4–2 victory. In the finale, David Ortiz got the Sox started with a 2-run first inning homer. And Johnny Damon, mired in a horrible 3-for-29 slump entering the game, drove the last nails in the Yankees' coffin with his second-inning grand slam and 2-run homer in the fourth, leading the Sox to a 10–3 victory in Yankee Stadium, on, of all days, Mickey Mantle's birthday. It was the first time in 137 tries that a major league team had won a series after trailing 3-games-to-none — the greatest comeback in baseball history.

101 A Reason to Believe

Curt Schilling, Keith Foulke, Pedro Martinez, and Derek Lowe. Johnny Damon, Mark Bellhorn, Manny Ramirez, and David Ortiz. Orlando Cabrera, Jason Varitek, Trot Nixon, Bill Mueller, and Kevin Millar. Owner John Henry and GM Theo Epstein. Manager Terry Francona. And all the rest of the Boston Red Sox. Twenty-five guys, one incredible team. The 2004 World Champions. Believe it.

10 Reasons to Hate the Yankees

Okay, so hate might be a strong word. Or maybe not strong enough. But at the very least, here are 10 reasons to really, really, really dislike the Yankees. And this is just a start.

1 George Steinbrenner

The long-time Yankees owner, and emperor of the Evil Empire, is the spoiled rich kid who gets whatever he wants. Despised throughout much of baseball for his free-spending ways and win-at-any-cost philosophy, no one is loathed more in Red Sox Nation.

2 Yankees Fans

They have this warped sense of entitlement. The Yankees have won so many world championships now that their fans believe it is their birthright to win each and every one. And they're arrogant. Yankees fans think they're so superior. Like the Yankees' success somehow makes them better people!

3 The Babe Ruth Deal

The Sox got some cash and the curse. The Yankees got the best player ever and the birth of a dynasty.

4 Roger Clemens

Not only did former Sox great Clemens win two World Series with the Yankees a few years after leaving Boston, but he wants to be inducted into the Hall of Fame wearing a Yankees cap.

5 Bucky "Bleepin'" Dent

The light-hitting Yankee shortstop homered off Boston starter Mike Torrez in the seventh inning of the 1978 do-or-die playoff game, giving the Yanks a 3-2 lead. The Yankees went on to win the game 5-4 and deny the Sox a berth in the World Series, prolonging the on-going misery in Red Sox Nation.

6 Aaron "Bleepin'" Boone

Boone was 5-for-31 in the 2003 ALCS when he hit his game-and-series-winning walk-off home run off Tim Wakefield in the bottom of the 11th-inning of Game 7, bringing another Red Sox season to a tragic conclusion.

7 Jeff Nelson and Karim Garcia

Yankee pitcher Nelson, and outfielder Garcia were accused of attacking a boisterous Fenway Park groundskeeper during Game 3 of the 2003 ALCS.

8 Piniella, Rivers, and Nettles

In 1976, Lou Piniella's knees-first collision with Sox catcher Carlton Fisk initiated a bench-clearing brawl that resulted in Sox pitcher Bill Lee being sucker punched by Mickey Rivers, and then thrown to the ground by Graig Nettles. Lee tore ligaments in his shoulder and missed two months of the season.

9 The A-Rod Deal

Shortly after the highly publicized near-trade of superstar Alex Rodriguez to Boston from Texas fell through, George Steinbrenner engineered his own mega-million dollar deal to bring A-Rod to the Yanks.

10 26 World Championships...Nuf Ced

Acknowledgments

First and foremost, a special word of thanks goes out to Leslie Stoker, Beth Huseman, Galen Smith, and all the folks at Stewart, Tabori & Chang for believing in the Red Sox, and the passion and devotion both I and Red Sox Nation feel for our favorite team.

I would also like to thank my dear friend (and art director), Mary Tiegreen, who conceived this series of books and continues to hit it out of the park with each and every book she's a part of.

To Kevin O'Sullivan at AP Wide World, Bill Burdick and staff at the National Baseball Hall of Fame Library, Aaron Schmidt in the Print Department of the Boston Public Library, Richard A. Johnson of the Sports Museum of New England, Brian Riley at Photofile, and Meghan McClure of the Boston Red Sox Public Relations Department, thank you for all your time and effort.

Thanks to Chip Bergstrom and Jim Tobin of River Communications for their suggestions and submission of materials, and Fred Pfannenstiehl for his insights and experiences as a life-long fan.

And, to my team, Mary, Savannah, Dakota, and Sam; my parents Ron and Beth; brother Ron (despite his Yankees affiliation); sister Edie; and the rest of the Greens, McGlones, and Mathwichs, I couldn't have done it without you. Thanks.

Manny Ramirez

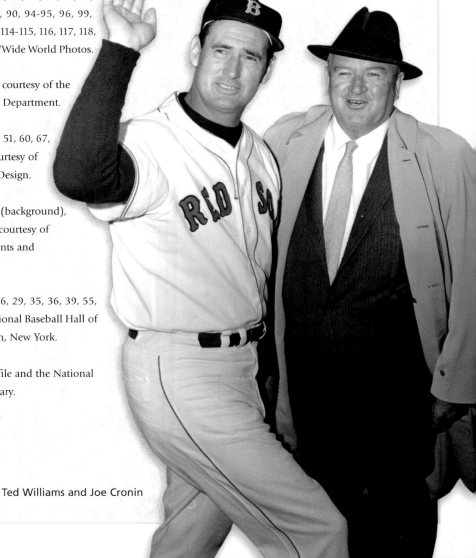

Photo Credits

Ted Williams and Joe Cronin

Stewart, Tabori & Chang
An imprint of Harry N. Abrams, Inc.

 A Tiegreen Book

101 Reasons to Love the Red Sox is a book in the
101 REASONS TO LOVE™ Series.

101 REASONS TO LOVE™ is a trademark of Mary
Tiegreen and Hubert Pedroli.

with the Library of Congress
101 Reasons to Love the Red Sox
ISBN 13: 978-1-58479-402-8
ISBN 10: 1-58479-402-X

Editor: Beth Huseman
Designer: David Green, Brightgreen Design
Production Manager: Jane Searle

The text of this book was composed in ITC Giovanni,
ITC New Baskerville, ITC Cheltenham, and Frutiger.

Printed and bound in China

10 9 8 7 6

harry n. abrams, inc.
a subsidiary of La Martinière Groupe
115 West 18th Street
New York, NY 10011
www.hnabooks.com